Step Into Your
MILLIONS

LENORE DEPP

authorHOUSE®

AuthorHouse™
1663 Liberty Drive
Bloomington, IN 47403
www.authorhouse.com
Phone: 833-262-8899

Published by AuthorHouse   03/18/2022

ISBN: 978-1-6655-5173-1 (sc)
ISBN: 978-1-6655-5177-9 (e)

Library of Congress Control Number: 2022903793

Print information available on the last page.

Contents

Section 1-4 Prosperity

Section 6-19 Gaining Wealth

Section 20-37 Getting Your Business Started

Bonus Section: Creating A Business Plan

Section 44-49 Spiritual Motivation

Dedication

I would like to take this opportunity to first and foremost thank my Lord and Savior Jesus Christ for giving me this vision and showing me how to put together this Stepping into Your Millions book. From pen to paper He led me and guided me throughout the writing process, giving me the words to use as well as the design of the book. God truly is amazing and his blessings are unmeasurable. And with that…. I say to God thank you! "Thank you, Father, for allowing millions of people to be blessed by this manuscript". "In the Mighty Name of Jesus Christ.

Introduction Come on let's Step Into Your MiLLIONS!

Have you ever noticed that nothing ever gets done when you procrastinate or wait on someone else to do it? The trouble is unless you take action immediately you might just look up to find that opportunity has now passed you by! Maybe you told yourself the time wasn't right. Or you want to be in a better place financially before you make any sudden life changes. Or, maybe you feel you won't get the support from your close friends or family members.

Bottom line, there is no better time than the present to pursue your dreams and reach for the stars! It's so easy to become complacent in where we are in life. If it's not broken don't fix it right? Wrong. Sometimes we need to break out of our comfort zone to step into our destiny!

If you're not chasing your goal you'll never move into the next phase of your life. Never let an opportunity pass you by. If you do it may never come around again. Here's the thing, at some point in life we get presented with incredible opportunities. The challenging part is having the courage to grab hold of the opportunity when it presents itself to you. You have the opportunity to learn firsthand how to become a millionaire! Becoming a millionaire doesn't have to be a dream. It can be your reality! If you want it. The only thing stopping you from reaching this goal is you.

People who take action achieve success. Additionally, these same individuals never let an opportunity pass them by. In this book, you will be given the tools to start a business that could lead you down the road of becoming a millionaire! I will show you that with a little faith, positive thinking, determination, a business plan, and spiritual guidance, nothing is impossible if you put in the work!

Prosperity Is Waiting on You!

Whenever you think of prosperity what comes to mind? Money, wealth, good fortune? If you thought of any of these terms, then you have the right mindset! Prosperity comes in many different forms; health, wealth, relationships, family, and life. One could want prosperity in terms of good health. Another could want to be prosperous in establishing good relationships with people they connect with. One might be prosperous in wealth, while others might be prosperous in other ways. The bottom line is…I THINK IT SAFE TO SAY, BEING PROSPEROUS IS SOMETHING MANY OF US WANT! No matter what that looks like to us individually.

In a nutshell, prosperity means different things to different people. For example, improving your relationship with your children and looking out for their happiness and well-being can bring prosperity your way. When you start doing things to bring prosperity, you will begin to see good happen. Having a spirit of prosperity is like seeing magic work in your life. You may meet a stranger who will say something to you that may spark an idea. Before you know it, that idea has grown into something much bigger than you could have ever imagined!

Beware of people who come around you with bad energy. Having prosperity makes others want to take from you. But don't worry they can't. Your spiritual sword will fight them off and keep them away! Thus, making you invulnerable.

Good Health & Prosperity

Prosperity to most people means being wealthy. Having more money than you know what to do with. No financial burdens or debts to worry about. Who wouldn't want that? But prosperity is not just about wealth. Prosperity is all around completeness. Whatever that may be for you! With that being said, let's look at prosperity in terms of good health. Did you know that it's God's will for us to be prosperous in all things? "Beloved, I pray that you may prosper in all things and be in health, just as your soul prospers. "(John chapter 3, 2nd verse) There are some people who would argue that choosing health over wealth is much more valuable in life. Others may argue the opposite. They would choose wealth instead of health. Either way, being prosperous in good health can make for a fulfilling life!

Wealth & Prosperity

Another form of prosperity is wealth. Which by "definition", *is an* accumulation of valuable economic resources that can be measured in terms of either real goods or money value.... Unlike income, which is a flow variable, wealth measures the amount of valuable economic goods that have been accumulated at a given point in time. So, why is financial wealth important? Building wealth has always been an important part of household financial stability. But with the typical family's wage income growing slowly and capital's role in the economy growing larger, owning productive assets and minimizing debt has never been more important for families' financial success. Being able to obtain and sustain financial freedom is how people would define having prosperity in wealth.

Relationships' In Regards to Prosperity

Even the dictionary makes this implication when it defines Prosperous/Prosperity as — Having success; Flourishing; Enjoying financial security; Propitious: Favorable. The core meaning of the word is "enjoying steady good fortune or financial security."

Can one have relationship prosperity? Even though we seldomly think to use the word in this term, I say we can. To understand Prosperity as it relates to relationships, however, we need to listen to and understand the word in a new way. To have relationship prosperity is to be fulfilled and have success with people with whom we connect. Have you ever met someone who has what seems to be all the money in the world, and yet they are the unhappiest? Thus, the phrase.... money can't buy love! Or happiness for that matter. For example, you may live in a nice house or drive a nice car, but your marriage or your relationship could be toxic or even dangerous. You could be in an abusive relationship and yet possess all the material things in the world. For this reason, I would much rather be rich in terms of love, and healthy relationships than money when it comes to this type of prosperity.

Family Prosperity

So, you may be wondering how prosperity relates to family? Well, let me briefly explain. To most of us, family is the most important thing in our lives. Family is the very core of our existence. Understanding that prosperity means more than financial wealth, it's not strange to want deep committed human relationships. This includes family. Being rich does not mean just money or material things. You could be rich in your love life, health, or happiness. A poor man once said, "I don't own a house on a hill, drive a fancy car, wear expensive clothes, or have a pocket full of money." But I'm rich nonetheless because I have a family that possesses everything I need." Therefore, I want for nothing." This is the true meaning of having family prosperity. Another way to look at prosperity concerning the family is the financial legacy and good fortune you want to pass on. The choices your loved ones make could greatly affect the success or downfall of your financial wealth.

Life Prosperity

Being prosperous in life means you are successful in everything you set out to accomplish. It means you're striving to make your world a better place, by helping others prosper along the way. People make the mistake of thinking that obtaining a prosperous life means you have to be wealthy and successful. But that is not necessarily true Waking up every day with a great attitude, positive mindset, and a determination to make the day be the best day it can be in my opinion is a success. The first and foremost thing to realize is that success is not just about achievement or the final result. Instead, it is the perseverance, the determination, the journey, the goal, and the vision. It's an amazing feeling to live a full life with no regrets. Embracing the ups and downs, accepting the triumphs and failures, meeting life's challenges, and walking bravely into your destiny. It's never too late in life to maximize your potential so you can achieve all that life has to offer!

What You Need to Have to Obtain Wealth

(Deuteronomy 8:18) But thou shalt remember the Lord thy God: for it is he that giveth thee power to get wealth, that he may establish his covenant which he sware unto thy fathers, as it is this day.

It is easy to dream of becoming a millionaire. However, it is a lot harder to obtain that kind of status when you don't know what it takes to achieve it. Well, I have just the tools you'll need to help make this dream a reality! If you are willing to do the work then you have already won half the battle! Over the next few sections of this booklet, I will touch on some important principles to follow about obtaining wealth.

Let's begin with patience. Having success does not happen overnight usually. Yes, there are special circumstances where an individual does something amazing or unique, and just like that, they've become an overnight success. I am not speaking about those instances. I am speaking to the average joe who dreams of success yet rushes too quickly to get to the finish line without pacing himself along the way.

There is no such thing as a quick get-rich plan. It takes time, discipline, and hard work to build wealth. One has to be patient enough to stick to whatever financial plan has been put together to ensure the long term will pay off in the end.

Next, let's look at persistence and how it relates to obtaining wealth. Building wealth is a fast process. You have to take your time, come up with a plan, and strategize ways to make that plan work. Most importantly you have to stick with it! No matter what. To be persistent is to be determined. You must stay focused on the end goal, versus what others are doing.

Work hard and maintain a consistent approach. This may not be easy, but it's doable for most people if they choose to make a commitment and stick to it. It is essential to know that anything you are passionate about requires patience and persistence. A lot of times people give up before they see the results if they don't feel it's going to work. Be careful because sometimes fear can block your reasons for being persistent. It can bring doubt, worry, and uncertainty. Persistence is the key to any successful endeavor. Keep doing it consistently for a very long time without giving up.

Being persistent also means having <u>determination.</u> Having determination means you are willing to do whatever is necessary to real your million-dollar status despite any challenges that may occur along the way. Like any goal, we set for ourselves at the beginning were excited, motivated, and ready to make it happen. However, somewhere along the way, we lose that ambition along with the determination to meet the goals we set for ourselves. After you make a firm decision to proceed on a task or goal, you may run into roadblocks and obstacles. If you have learned the rule that you should be determined to achieve that goal, you will focus your energy and efforts on sticking with it until the job is done! This is where <u>ambition </u>comes into play.

Ambitious people have a gleam in their eyes as they approach reaching their goals. Ambition is the driving force behind individuals seeking to accomplish whatever it is they set out to achieve. But what does that have to do with obtaining wealth? Ambitious people know what they want and they have clear goals and work very hard to accomplish them. So, someone wanting to be a millionaire embraces challenges with a determined mindset to win at any cost because this is what they want.

To achieve success ambitious people, take charge of their destiny and don't expect others to bow down to their needs. They have willpower and determination. They know where they are going and what they have to do to get there. They are capable of changing and measuring up to their dreams, always watchful of the opportunities that are out there for those who are willing to see them and seize them. If you can see it you can dream it. If you can dream it, you can achieve it. Determination brings <u>motivation.</u>

Motivation is what gets the gears going when wanting to become a millionaire. However, motivation alone is not enough. It takes discipline, hard work, sacrifice, and a willingness to "grab the bull by the horns"

and take charge of your financial success. It's one thing to have big dreams but without passion, those dreams don't go anywhere. Once you've decided you are going to be wealthy, you have to determine your reason for wanting this financial success. And that means determining you're why. Your why drives a deep sense of purpose and helps you develop the motivation you need. This then leads to putting together a financial plan that could potentially be a success.

Remember this important note; "Motivation reflects something unique about each one of us and allows us **to gain valued outcomes like improved performance, enhanced well-being, personal growth**, or a sense of purpose." Motivation is a pathway to change our way of thinking, feeling, and pursuing wealth. No matter what it is you want to be successful in it takes having a little <u>faith</u> to get the ball rolling.

It's easy to have faith in your dream in the beginning and near the end of the journey. But when the initial excitement wears off, and the end is nowhere in sight, things may sometimes appear quite bleak. Therefore, without realizing it time has passed and that dream has now become a faint memory. Unfortunately, when facing the challenges of becoming wealthy, most people quit before their dream has had time to become a reality.

This is something that happens to most people who start strong and jump feet first into the pool of opportunity. Have you ever heard the saying nothing you want comes easy? It's true! Being aware that challenges are a natural part of the goal-achieving process helps you stick with them and meet them with success.

Instead of focusing on the problem, as most people do, use your imagination to picture what you want. Instead of sinking into despair and thinking your dreams are impossible, remember that the idea in your heart is already in route.

And above all, instead of abandoning your dream, understand that it's important to give all you've got to the task that's in front of you. Even if, you have no idea what's coming next. Believe in your dreams, believe in yourself, and believe the impossible can be possible if you carry a little faith with you along the journey!

Getting Rid of Things That Hinder Reaching Your Wealth

(Deuteronomy 22:9) "You shall not sow your vineyard with two kinds of seed, or all the produce of the seed which you have sown and the increase of the vineyard will become defiled.

Most of us, have negative stuff that gets in the way of achieving wealth. If you can abandon these habits, only then can you understand that **becoming a millionaire** is not as far from reality as you think. Fear, unforgiveness, doubt, and negativity are the biggest hindering blocks that can keep us stuck and stagnated. Starting with fear. It is one thing to say that you want to become a millionaire and quite another to start doing it. If you want to get out of financial stagnation, then you need to act as soon as possible.

Meaning, putting away any fears you have aside to move forward in conquering your mission to becoming a millionaire. Another downside to having fear is staying in your comfort zone because you fear taking risks. Most people fear the unknown. And let's face it taking a chance on something as big as being a millionaire is scary within itself. This brings me to the next negative factor doubt.

One of the greatest obstacles that hinder humans from fulfilling their dreams is self-doubt. Self-doubt is what almost all of us struggle with from time to time. AND-it's something we can all relate too right? Whether it's from our own experience or from someone we know. Self-doubt can be harmful not only to your overall well-being it can also be harmful to your accomplishments and the goals you set for your life. Self-doubt also creates procrastination.

Procrastination may seem harmless at first, but when self-doubt begins to creep in and you're consistently starting without moving beyond that then you'll begin a long cycle of procrastination that will prevent you from getting anything done.

Including establishing a business that could bring you potential wealth. Hesitation is one of the grandchildren of self-doubt. When people are hesitant about doing something, they procrastinate until they miss out on that opportunity and find an excuse to justify themselves for not taking advantage of that opportunity.

Another negative hindering block that is not all that common to a lot of people is unforgiveness. What is unforgiveness? Unforgiveness is holding a grudge against someone who has wronged you. This then leads to bitterness against others. Having unforgiveness is not good for two reasons. The first reason is, it impacts us negatively, emotionally, mentally, physically, financially, and spiritually. The longer we hold a grudge the heavier that burden is to carry. And trust and know it carries a heavyweight. Unforgiveness can cause you to be unproductive, fearful of trusting your instincts, unable to function or focus on a task, and perhaps a lack of direction and sense of purpose.

Secondly, unforgiveness can prevent the growth we need to succeed in being the best version of ourselves. Unforgiveness affects our character and integrity as grudges do not bring out the best in us. Additionally, Unforgiveness also compromises our physical health. Research has shown that unforgiveness is connected to high blood pressure, weakened immune systems, reduced sleep, chronic pain, and cardiovascular problems.

On another note, did you know that unforgiveness comes in between you and the heavenly father? (God) Unforgiveness affects your spirit and your soul, hindering your spiritual growth and fruitfulness. You may feel spiritually dry, stuck, or stalled in your spiritual life. Unforgiveness hinders you from receiving all that God has for you. How we can expect God to open up the windows of heaven and pour us out blessings when we can't forgive those who may have wronged us. For this reason, we need to forgive so that we can move forward. The one common denominator all of these obstacles have is negativity.

Negativity no matter what angle it comes from can be our biggest downfall. Misery loves company! The more we welcome that type of energy into our lives, into our business, into our relationships, the more we find ourselves accepting that negativity and owning it. We have to be careful of the company we keep. To be successful in life surrounding yourself with positive energy is key. You want to be around people who are seeking the same things you are. People who are ambitious, motivated, self-driven, and like-minded. You only hold yourself back when we entertain individuals who do not share the same interest as us we do, or the same passions and dreams, they become a stumbling block for us. They hold no place or value in our space. Therefore, they end up being an unnecessary problem. This goes for friendships, relationships, business relationships, and family. Remember this, positive energy brings positive results. Negative energy brings negative results.

Giving Is the Key to Your Wealth

You may be wondering…… how does giving lead to wealth? The Holy Scriptures provide us with a guide on how to obtain wealth. The words of God do not only include instructions on how to save our soul, but they also teach us important lessons to avoid poverty on Earth. If you want to prosper in life, then God has given us a road map to follow to obtain riches on earth, AND favor with him. There are scriptures in the Bible that teach us the principles to get wealth. Therefore, we must possess these qualities to receive the wealth and blessings that God promised us. **Deuteronomy 8:18** But remember the LORD your God, for it is he who gives you the ability to produce wealth, and so confirms his covenant, which he swore to your ancestors, as it is today. (NIV)

Sowing a Seed Through Giving of Our Time

There are various ways in which we can be givers. For starters, one can be a giver of their time. Giving someone your time sometimes means more than giving them monetary gifts. Spending time with people who are special to us shows how much we value and appreciate the place they hold in our hearts. Being accessible to a friend in need is another example of giving a person your time. As we journey through life and experience the difficulties and challenges that occur, knowing we have a friend who is only a phone call away can make all the difference in the world. When we are givers of our time, we are sowing a spiritual seed into the earth of goodwill toward one another.

Romans 12:9-13 Let love be genuine. Abhor what is evil; hold fast to what is good. Love one another with brotherly affection. Outdo one another in showing honor. Do not be slothful in zeal, be fervent in spirit, serve the Lord. Rejoice in hope, be patient in tribulation, be constant in prayer. Contribute to the needs of the saints and seek to show hospitality.

Sowing a Seed of Giving in Services

Perhaps one of the most overlooked ways of giving is giving in services to others. So, what exactly does this mean? It simply means putting the needs of others before your own. In other words, looking out for someone who is in need or needs your help. Putting other people's needs before yours strengthens your relationships. It can bring people together and create a special bond with them. Remember when Hurricane Katrina happened some years ago and brought destruction and devastation to New Orleans? This was such a dark time for many of the surviving residents that lived there. However, the beautiful thing that came out of that gloomy time, was the people themselves. People from around the world volunteered their services to help families that were homeless, left without food or water, and clothing. Because of their generosity in giving their services, New Orleans has been rebuilt and is still thriving! Sowing a seed of giving in services means you can reap a harvest in receiving all the blessings God has for you.

Proverbs 19:23 Each man should give what he has decided in his heart to give, not reluctantly or under compulsion, for God loves a cheerful giver. Each man should give what he has decided in his heart to Each man should give what he has decided in his heart

Proverbs 22:9 The generous will themselves be blessed, for they share their food with the poor. he

Lending a helping hand is one of the easiest things you can do to make a difference in this world. You can improve the world, one day, one person, and one act of kindness at a time.

Sowing a Seed in Giving to Donations, Charities, and Ministries

Donating to charities is a wonderful way of giving back to institutions that are in the business of helping others. Why is this important in reference to establishing wealth? According to the Bible; It is better to give than to receive. **Acts 20:35 (KJV)**

I have shown you all things, how that so laboring ye ought to support the weak, and to remember the words of the Lord Jesus, how he said, It is more blessed to give than to receive.

In other words, it is more rewarding to give than it is to get something back. Think of it as a way of paying it forward looking for no expectations in return. Donating to the causes you care about not only benefits the charities themselves, but it can also **be deeply rewarding for you too**. Millions of people give to charity regularly to support causes they believe in, as well as for the positive effect it has on their own lives. Most importantly, giving to charities, donations, and churches is how we are blessed in other areas of our lives. The more we give to others the more we receive blessings!

Remember, giving from your heart is an act of kindness that can't be measured or valued necessarily in dollars or cents. It's measured by love and a willingness to help those in need as well as those who are doing the work of being a good servant. This would include giving to church ministries that support their communities, youth programs, families in financial hardships, public schools on tight budgets and can barely afford books and other materials for their students due to lack of funds, and of course, elderly people who may be alone or suffering health issues.

2 Corinthians 9:10 King James Bible: Now he that ministereth seed to the sower both minister bread for *your* food, and multiply your seed sown, and increase the fruits of your righteousness;)

Fear Can Be Your Road Block

Fear is a powerful force. It helps us stay alive and prevents us from doing stupid stuff. However, it's also a very limiting mental blockade that can prevent you from achieving the life you want. Fear has the power to rob you of your ambitions, goals, and dreams. Fear creates excuses that seem legitimate enough so that you'll stop chasing your dream and eventually go back to your comfort zone.

Fear of Rejection

The fear of rejection is probably the biggest fear many of us can relate to. It's the one fear I'll be discussing that can lead to other fears. At one time or another, we've all experienced some form of rejection in our lives. Whether it was rejection from an elite college, job interview, or by someone of interest. Either way, rejection hurts. It makes us feel inadequate. It lowers our self-esteem and confidence. In some cases, it can hurt so bad that people might even slip into depression.

Unfortunately, the fear of rejection causes many people to give up on their dreams and ambitions. Therefore, they don't grab every opportunity that comes their way. They don't start a business because they're afraid they won't get the support of their friends and family or have the resources or finances to get started. And let's face it if you tell yourself enough times you'll fail before you even get started, you'll convenience yourself that it's true. Not realizing you are setting up your self-destruction. Remember words have power! Life and power lye's in the power of the tongue.

I once read somewhere that "there is nothing to fear, but fear itself". (Franklin D Roosevelt 1933 inaugural address). I couldn't agree more. Fearing anything or anyone is never a good feeling. Don't misunderstand me fear does have its place. And therefore, in those cases it causes us to respond when we feel we're in danger or in harm's way. However, in any given situation we mustn't give fear permission to run our lives or hold us back!

Fear of Failure

Let's look at another type of fear that's not all that unfamiliar. The fear of failure. the fear of failure can be so paralyzing that people simply decide to procrastinate over and over again, even though they continue talking about their goals. The fear of failure is another big reason why people don't achieve the success of living their best lives. Just the thought of failing at something will keep you, prisoner, to your negative thoughts.

The reward for procrastinating is that you protect yourself from 'real' failure. Because as long as you don't put in the necessary effort for success, you're at least not confronted by 'real' failure. You can still refer back to the excuse that you haven't given it your all because you are just not sure if you can. Unfortunately, that's simply not true and you potentially can do so much more if you believe you can. Please know one thing for sure. **Not taking action is a bigger failure than 'failing' at your goals.**

When you fail at your goal, despite taking action, you'd still learn valuable lessons and therefore grow. However, if you simply give in to those failures you won't learn the lesson you needed to get from that failure. The important thing to remember is that on your journey to success you must fail and make mistakes. It's an essential part of the process. Therefore, it is during those moments, you'll learn new valuable lessons that'll help you get closer to your end goal.

Fear of Success

The fear of success is a type of fear that most people wouldn't think of as a roadblock in terms of success. After all who in their right mind would be afraid of succeeding? Sounds crazy I know. But rest assured, the fear of success is very much a real thing! And it happens to people more often than you think. Success to some people is scary. Walking into your success can be frightening. After all, it's unknown territory. And we all can agree that we fear what is unknown to us.

Maybe you're afraid of success because you fear your friends or family will reject you if you have a different lifestyle compared to them. Or possibly hate you just on the strength of success alone. It's not easy wearing the suit of success! There's a level of confidence that comes over a person when they put this type of suit on. Causing others to envy your success and therefore you become a target of their jealousy in unfortunate ways.

Additionally, Maybe you fear success because you know you'll have to leave some old friends behind who don't share the same ambitions and goals in life as you do. Which can lead to rejection by certain people in your social circle. Or, maybe you fear success because you're afraid of having more responsibilities and expectations put on you. Maybe you fear success because you don't feel worthy of obtaining success. Maybe you have been told your whole life you'll never be anything, or go anywhere and that's what you've believed.

If you can relate to any of these types of fears, you are not alone. The important thing is that you identify and accept them. Only then you'll be able to conquer and overcome them.

Fear of Ridicule

This is a more unique form of fear of rejection, but it's still a massive limiting factor for many people. Maybe you want to start a business that some of your friends or family don't understand. Or maybe you have certain interests that some of the people around you make fun of. In many cases, we fear that the things we do, say, or like will be ridiculed and made fun of by other people. This fear will be even bigger if it concerns the opinions of our friends and family.

There's nothing more disheartening than being excited to start something new only to have it crushed by negative "nellies". Meaning, the people who should support you only end up giving you all the reasons to not pursue what it is you are passionate about. Ridicule coming from friends and family can hurt more verses coming from strangers. It's hard enough stepping out of our comfort zone into unfamiliar territory. And with no support or encouragement, sometimes we won't even attempt it.

So how do we deal with the fear of ridicule? By first realizing you can't give in to that fear no matter what it may cost you. Secondly, if we focus less on fear and more on the dreams we want to see happen for us, then we can eliminate falling prey to it. Becoming fearless is not about fearing nothing — it's about feeling the fear and doing it anyway!

Taking Steps to Own your Business and Becoming a Successful Entrepreneur

Now that you've started thinking about your dream business and being that entrepreneur, you envisioned a million times over, it's time to ask the BIG question. WHAT NOW?....... You know what you want and how you want it, but what you don't know is where to start! Which is not uncommon when wanting to start a business. Most people have no idea how to take a passion and turn it into something successful. I too was once like that. I now have my own business and have been a successful entrepreneur for many years. In this section, I am going to teach you the necessary steps to take to own your business be a successful Entrepreneur! Are you ready to take the first step into your future? If the answer is yes! Then what are you waiting for? Let's go! Come on let's step!

Step 1 Create the Business You Want

With any business adventure, you start, it has to be something you are passionate about. If you are passionate about it, more than likely you'll put your all into it. Also, it doesn't hurt to have some knowledge about the business. The more insight you have the easier it will be to know what works or doesn't when you are in the planning stages. For example, maybe you want to start a cooking class business for beginners who want to learn the ins and outs of being an amazing chef. You would need to know your way around a kitchen. Along with having experience cooking various dishes that have received great reviews. I heard someone say… if you do what you love, you'll never work another day in your life. And let me tell you that is true! Don't misunderstand me, it's going to take work to start up a business. However, when it's a business you are excited about, it won't feel the same as going in every day and punching a time clock working for someone else. With that being said, let's keep stepping don't stop! You're on your way.

Step 2 Name Your Business

Your brand's (business) name is the nitch of your business. It represents the product or services your business is offering. The name must be **something that grabs the attention of the consumer.** It should resonate with your target audience.... In other words, a strong brand name is vital to establishing a strong brand reputation. Not to mention, a name makes a clear statement about your product. Therefore, it has to stand out! Millions of people buy certain brands because of the name. Take, for example, a pair of jeans are just jeans. But, put a name like Sean Jean (Puffy Combs) behind them, now those jeans mean something to customers. A bottle of perfume is just a bottle until you read the name Rhianna on it. It's all in the name!

Finally, the most important thing after naming your business is to protect it by registering your business name. Once you settle on a name you like, you need to protect it. There are four different ways to register your business name. Each way of registering your name serves a different purpose, and some may be legally required depending on your business structure and location.

- Entity name protects you at a state level
- Trademark protects you at a federal level
- Doing business as (DBA) doesn't give legal protection, but it might be legally required
- Domain name protects your business website address

Each of these name registrations is legally independent. Most small businesses try to use the same name for each kind of registration, but you're not normally required to.

Additionally, another step in this process of naming your business is the domain name. If you want an online presence for your business, start by registering a domain name — also known as your website address, or URL.

Once you register your domain name, no one else can use it for as long as you continue to own it. It's a good way to protect your brand presence online.

If someone else has already registered the domain you wanted to use, that's okay. Your domain name doesn't need to be the same as your legal business name, trademark, or DBA. You'll register your domain name through a registrar service. Consult a directory of accredited registrars to determine which ones are safe to use, and then pick one that offers you the best combination of price and customer service. You'll need to renew your domain registration yearly to keep it active.

I know it seems like a lot to do to get started, but you've got this! Let's keep stepping! You are closer than you realize to making this happen!

Step 3 Decide if Your Business Will Be an LLC, Scorp, or CCorp

Before starting your business, you want to decide which corporation would be best to put your business under. Such as LLC, Scorp, or CCorp. you may be asking yourself...why is that important? Let's start with learning the difference between a corporation and an LLC. The one commonality found with these two is that both protect owners so they're not personally on the hook for business liabilities or debts.

Key differences include how they're owned (LLCs have one or more individual owners and corporations have shareholders) and maintained (corporations generally have more formal record-keeping and reporting requirements). Even though LLCs are considered easier to start and maintain, investors tend to prefer corporations.

The difference between a C corporation and an S corporation is the way you're taxed and owned, and how shares work.

C corporation income is taxed twice—the business pays taxes on its net income, and then the shareholders also pay taxes on the profits they receive. With S corporation income, only the shareholders pay taxes on profits received.

C corporations have no limits on how many people and who can own shares. S corporations are limited to 100 shareholders who must be U.S. citizens or residents.

C corporation owners may get preferred stock—which comes with no voting rights but priority to dividends before common shareholders. S corporation owners can only get common stock which comes with voting rights. Let's continue stepping! The journey is not over yet!

Step 4 Register with the Secretary OF State

Congrats! You've decided to take the next big step in entrepreneurship and start making your business a legal enterprise. Many small business owners need to register with their Secretary of State. Are you one of them? If you are, then the following information will be helpful to you!

Generally speaking, all corporations, limited liability companies, and limited liability partnerships need to register with their state. If you secure the help of a lawyer or legal forms company to set up the legal structure of your business, this step should be included. It is always a good idea, however, to give your state office a call and see if there are special steps for your jurisdiction that may be out of the norm. While a lawyer in your state should be well-versed on the rules, it's ultimately your responsibility to have everything completed.

There are some states, counties, and municipalities that may also have regulations regarding who can do business in their jurisdiction. They may require a specific business license or permit for everything from hair services to computer repair, and often a state business registration can provide the documentation needed for application — or even hasten the processing of the permit.

The very first thing that is recommended for any business to do is to contact their state office. A quick Google search for your state name and "Secretary of State" should give you the right link. (Be sure you are looking at a site that ends in ".gov" and not an advertised listing or for-profit site.) Your state's site should have the relevant info for you in their FAQ's or a special business owner's section of the website.

If it's not easy to find, or you are not confident that the data is the most updated, you should give their office a call. (Recent regulations in your state may have changed registration requirements. A live agent will be aware of any discrepancies on the website.) If the entire process can be completed online, be prepared to provide the following information:

- Your business name (or desired name, if not previously registered)
- The person responsible for business (owner, partner, or point of contact)
- Business start date
- Business type
- Legal entity type (S-corp, LLC, partnership, etc.)
- Basic contact details

Some states will also allow you to create a state tax number, or require one that has already been created. Many states provide the registration free of charge and will give you confirmation of your application submission immediately. For states that do charge an application or business filing fee, you may have the option to pay online with a checking account, credit, or debit card. Others may ask that you mail in payment with a printed invoice.

Still excited? Of course, you are! You've come this far so let's keep going! Let's step into the next phase of your business.

Step 5 Contact the IRS and Get Your EIN Number

So what does it mean to contact the IRS and get an EIN number? Your state tax ID and federal tax ID numbers — also known as an Employer Identification Number (EIN) — work such as a personal social security number, but for your business. They let your small business pay state and federal taxes. Your Employer Identification Number (EIN) is your federal tax ID. You need it to pay federal taxes, hire employees, open a bank account, and apply for business licenses and permits. It's free to apply for an EIN, and you should do it right after you register your business. Your business needs a federal tax ID number if it does any of the following:

- Pays employees
- Operates as a corporation of partnership
- Files tax returns for employment, excise, or alcohol, tobacco, and firearms
- Withholds taxes on income, other than wages, paid to a non-resident alien
- Uses a Keogh Plan (a tax-deferred pension plan)
- Works with certain types of organizations

Apply for an EIN with the IRS assistance tool. It will guide you through questions and ask for your name, social security number, address, and your "doing business as" (DBA) name. Your nine-digit federal tax ID becomes available immediately upon verification.

Step 6 Create a Professional E-Mail for Your Business

Having a business email address **shows customers you are a legitimate business**. Sending emails with your business name allows you to promote your brand with each email you send. Additionally, it separates your personal life from your business. Because there are so many fake businesses created to scam innocent people like you or me, having a professional e-mail linked to your business maintains a professional image.

In business, continuing a professional image is important for gaining your customers' trust and being credible online. When future customers contact you with questions, or if you reach out to them or other businesses, having an e-mail address that looks professional with your email through your business's domain name represents that your business is well-established and genuine. Thus, making customers feel more comfortable dealing with you. Which is what you want when promoting your business to the public.

So far so good! Let's continue stepping! It takes determination to get to where you want to be!

Step 7 Get a Business Phone Number

It is important to have a business phone number for the following reasons. Regardless of whether you own a small or big business, having a business phone number works wonders. **It gives your business credibility and works to promote the name and image of your company**. It also does not give you a problem when you plan to shift base. You need a **phone number for your business that strictly operates during your business hours**. Having designated business hours is one of the greatest reasons to have a dedicated line to your company. This way, when anyone calls you at the end of your workday, they can be greeted with a message.

Additionally, having a business phone number prevents your phone line from being tied up and missing important calls. There's nothing worse than taking a personal call that could cause you to miss out on gaining a new client, or job proposition because you were not reachable.

Step 8 Create a Professional Website for Your Business

Creating a website for your business is a great way to attract people. The more creative and exciting you make your website; the more customers will be drawn to it. And isn't that the whole point? In today's society, everything we do is on the internet. From searching on google to online dating apps to following various social media platforms, the internet is where everyone goes. Additionally, having your website lets you create a branded email address which adds a level of professionalism to all of your correspondence, especially if you've used a personal email address to conduct business up until now.

Also, having a professional website showcases your products and services. Based on the content that's on your website, this is how potential customers learn who you are as the business owner and what it is you offer that is appealing to them. A website can also encourage customers to reach out to you if they are interested in purchasing your products. More importantly, if your website looks professional it then makes a great impression and gives people comfort that you are a legit business. Last but not least, when you establish a professional website, it can be used as a great marketing tool for not only your business but for other businesses who may want to know more about you.

Hang in there! You are almost home! So, come on let's keep Stepping! You don't have that far to go!

Step 9 Create a Professional Greeting

When you are a business owner you'll want to establish a greeting that makes your customers want to do business with you! Since first impressions generally reflect how people may see us upon first glance you'll want to show your best side. Hence, when your customers contact you, you shouldn't respond with a greeting as if you were talking to your girl pal or frat brother from college. Greetings set the tone for your business.

They influence how your audience perceives you. If you were going out on a date with someone you've never met you wouldn't want their first impression of you to be an awful one. In other words, you probably wouldn't show up in wrinkling clothes hair, not groomed, with a five-o clock shadow because you haven't shaved (if you're a guy) in weeks. That would probably be the first and the last time you'll go out with them again.

Therefore, you'll want to capitalize on your opportunity to make an excellent first impression in all of your professional means of communication. Also, a greeting is a way of showing a person you see them and you acknowledge their presence. It also makes clear that you are there to help if they need it.

Do not underestimate the power of phone greetings. You want a potential customer that calls to leave that conversation feeling that your business is a place they want to visit in person. The tone of voice is important when answering the phone. There is truth to the phrase "It's not what you say, but how you say it." That refers to tone also.

Step 10 Create Business Cards

Business cards are a great marketing tool when advertising your business. The business card **represents your company's brand**. Not only does it convey important personal contact information such as name, title, email, website, address, and phone number, but oftentimes it is also the first exposure to the overall image of the business. Sometimes in the hustle and bustle of the day, having your business cards on hand is a quick way to promote your business on the spot.

Now when it comes to you the business owner, you want to make sure your business cards look attractive and catchy. If your business card looks plain and boring, it may cause a potential client to toss it aside, never picking it up again. For this reason, you'll want to create business cards that are an immediate attention grabber.

Also, your business cards should contain the following information.

- Logo.
- Company name.
- Tagline.
- Your name.
- Job title.
- Website.
- Contact details.

You got this! Believe in yourself. Each step you take brings you closer to being that professional Entrepreneur! Come on let's keep stepping!

Step 11 Marketing Your Business

Marketing is **important because it helps you sell your products or services**. The bottom line of any business is to make money and marketing is an essential channel to reach that end goal. Without marketing, many businesses wouldn't exist because marketing is ultimately what drives sales. Think about the commercials we see every day of every minute marketing some type of product they're selling. Has this ever happened to you?

You are sitting on the couch or in your favorite chair and a commercial comes on advertising a juicy burger that melts in your mouth when you take a big bite into it. Then all of sudden, you realize it's dinner time and you haven't eaten yet. Now that burger you just saw on the TV. Sounds mighty tasty. You jump into your car and you're headed out to get that burger! That's marketing! How you market your business determines if the enterprise will be successful or not. Marketing is a tool used to create and maintain demand, relevance, reputation, competition, and more. Without it, your business is likely to close down due to a lack of sales.

Marketing is a tool that engages its customers in your business. Engaging involves furnishing your customers with relevant information about your products and your business as well. It's all about creating fresh content. After all, this is how you keep the customers interested in your marketing product. Social media is one of the best platforms where you can engage your customers. Since almost the whole world uses social media, it is nearly impossible for a business to not thrive or grow using this marketing tool.

Through your marketing, the customers get to know about the value of the products, their usage, and additional information that could be helpful to the customers. It creates brand awareness and makes the business stand out.

Step 12 Open Up a Business Account

When starting your business, you'll want to open a business account. This account will strictly be used for your business. A business bank account plays a key role in growing your business while protecting it and yourself at the same time. It **allows you to keep track of business expenses, simplify tax reporting, and deposit payments under your company name.** You'll want to do this as soon as your business gets up and running, and when you get an Employer Identification Number (EIN) or begin to accept or spend money. A business account will help you keep better track of what's coming in and going out regarding your expenses.

This is important because the Internal Revenue Service (IRS) requires that any incorporated business have a business bank account. The rule applies whether the business is structured as a sole partnership, a partnership, limited liability company (LLC), or corporation. It is equally important to know a business bank account is a prerequisite for obtaining business loans. The reason is that lenders won't approve your business loans unless funds can be deposited into a business bank account.

Additionally, a business bank account is a must if you want to accept credit card payments for merchandise or services. If you have an eCommerce business, you'll need a business bank account to accept payments through your point-of-sale system.

You're on your way to making this happen don't stop now! Let's continue stepping! I know you can do this.

Step 13 Seek Professional Guidance

Depending on what type of business you're wanting to start, it is always good practice to seek out professional guidance about state compliances when it comes to starting a business. Each state has different rules, regulations, and zoning laws. Many business rules and regulations vary from state to state. Therefore, to protect yourself and your business you'll want to be knowledgeable of what is or isn't permitted in your state. For example, maybe you'll want to start a hair salon business and you're not sure if the location is in a zone that prohibits having a business there. Knowing this information in advance could save you from losing your business license and possibly paying a hefty fine down the road.

It is important to follow risk governance and compliance with the relevant legislation. As well as maintaining the standards set by laws. The absence of proper governance risk and compliance according to the law, rules and regulations can affect business and can damage the reputation of the company and clients too. Hence, Business laws and legislations are the laws governing companies. They include those regulations associated with intellectual property, employment, insurance, business entity formation, and other matters. So, as you can see no matter what your business is to avoid legal problems take the time to research good professional advice before starting.

Step 14 Consult a Tax Advisor

Running a business can be hard work, time-consuming, and possibly a bit overwhelming. Not to mention, trying to handle the financial aspects as well. One more thing to deal with, right? This is where consulting a tax advisor comes in handy! So, what is a tax advisor? And what does he do? Glad you asked. A tax advisor is a tax consultant who can explain the different tax treatments of raising money by taking out loans versus selling part of the business to an investor. A tax accountant can even help plan the timing and amount of profit distributions and employee bonuses. Think of a tax advisor as a safety net for your business when it comes to financial revenues.

Also, a tax advisor can save you money, time, when dealing with the I.R.S, (Internal Revenue Services) give you peace of mind knowing someone else is handling your tax issues, advise you now and all year round on the best strategies to make smart tax-saving decisions, take look at your past returns to see if any deductions were missed and if so, amend them for you, and limit your risk of an audit.

Professional tax preparers are paid to keep up with the tax code and their expertise can help ensure that you get all the deductions and credits you are eligible to receive. I strongly anyone starting a business to do your homework and make sure the tax advisor you may be seeking out is creditable and professional.

With starting a business, the possibilities are endless! The sky is the limit and there is nothing you can't achieve if you believe you can! No time to give up now…. Come on let's keep stepping!

Types of Businesses Trending In the 21ˢᵗ Century

As of 2020 going into 2021 the world as we know it has drastically changed. Going into lockdown, social distancing, virtual learning, wearing a face mask, and vaccination shots is now our new "normal" Covid-19 came in and completely turned our world upside down. Schools shut down businesses were forced to close and for many people all around the world, the future seemed bleak, dark, and disparaging.

But the good news is…the world has embraced the new "norm" and slowly we are moving into a much brighter future. With that being said, millions of people have had to reach into their bags of creativity to start up a business. There are businesses out there trending that are neat and innovative. Below I have listed some of them.

01. Shifting toward eCommerce

In the past years, there's been a steady shift of brick and mortar stores taking their businesses and services online and launching successful eCommerce websites. Under the current climate, most small businesses are looking to eCommerce to create new opportunities through selling their merchandise online, either as their main source of income or in congruence with additional practices.

02. Mobile marketing

Mobile marketing is one of the biggest small business trends to take over the global stage with no indication of slowing down. It means marketing your business to your mobile user audience by reaching them via their smartphones or tablets.

03. Rolling out your app

More people are using their mobile devices to conduct daily transactions than ever before, from doing groceries to booking fitness classes. As a result, it might be time to pair your small business website with a mobile app of your very own.

Obtain Multiple Streams of Income

Starting a new business can bring lots of uncertainty. Such as, will the business I'm creating be productive? Will it be a success? Will my product be enough to gain attraction from customers? More importantly, will my business generate enough income to sustain the profits of what's coming in and going out? These are all questions many entrepreneurs may ask themselves. But no worries, I am here to put those thoughts to rest. I am briefly going to explain you should obtain multiple streams of income outside of your business.

Obtaining multiple streams of income is necessary because there are far too many different avenues accessible for making additional income. The one mistake people make is not taking advantage of those opportunities. Hence, here are a few reasons as to why you don't want to be one of those people who miss out. The first reason: If your business takes a while to bring in wealth, having other sources to get money can help you stay afloat during rough times.

Secondly, generating more than one source of income can bring more money to your household. Which can allow you to financially have the means to do other things. Thirdly, If your business suffers a loss, then at least you'll potentially be able to sustain from financially going under. And trust me when difficult times arise, you'll want to have something to fall back on. For all these reasons I just mentioned, please understand it is wise to obtain multiple streams of income outside of your main business.

Here are 13 Examples of Multiple Streams of Income

1. Wholesaling

2. Air BNB

3. Become a Professional Life Coach

4. Rent out your vehicle-Turo.com

5. Lyft-Delivery Services

6. Door Dash -Delivery Services

7. Housekeeping

8. Daycare Services

9. Start an Errand Service

10. Transportation Service

11. Invest in Stocks

12. Virtual Assistance

13. Tutoring Online Service

Bonus Section:
Creating A Business Plan

Creating a Business Plan

The Purpose of a Business Plan

A Business Plan helps you evaluate the feasibility of a new business idea in an objective, critical, and unemotional way.

- Marketing – Is there a market? How much can you sell?
- Management – Does the management team have the skill?
- Financial – Can the business make a profit?

It provides an **operating plan** to assist you in running the business and improves your probability of success.

- Identify opportunities and avoid mistakes
- Develop production, administrative, and marketing plans
- Create budgets and projections to show financial outcomes

It communicates your idea to others, serves as a "selling tool," and provides the basis for your financing proposal.

- Determine the amount and type of financing needed
- Forecast profitability and investor return on investment
- Forecast cash flow, show liquidity and ability to repay debt

Who will use the plan? If you won't use the plan to raise money, your plan will be internal and maybe less formal. If you are presenting it to outsiders as a financing proposal, presentation quality and thorough financial analysis is very important

Writing Out a Business Plan Outline

Writing out a Business Plan can take a lot of time. Possibly up to 100 hours or more. This is not uncommon for a new business that requires a lot of research.

When starting your business, you'll want to choose a plan that is tailored to your business. For this reason, you'll want to learn about the Traditional Business plan and the Lean-Startup Business plan. These are two business plans designed for small businesses. Both are important to have but provide different needs. It is up to you the business owner to decide which plan works for you.

A. Choose a Business Plan that fits Your Needs

    a) Traditional Business Plan
    b) Lean-Startup Business Plan

B. **Executive Summary**-; information you share with consumers detailing various aspects of what your company provides. It may include the following.

    c) Mission Statement
    d) Product Service
    e) Information highlighting employees' pieces of training or experiences, leadership skills, etc....
    f) Location
    g) Financial Information/High-level growth plans (If planning to seek financial assistance.)

C. **Company Description**- Your company's detailed description is an excellent way for consumers to know the following:

h) Ways your business solves consumer problems

i) How your company Identifies organizations, consumers, and businesses to which your company will provide services.

j) Details on why your business is a success as well as the advantages your company has over your competitors.

D. **Market Analysis** – To have a successful business it is important to know the industry of your company so that you can research what other companies are doing to be competitive. In your competitive research, you'll want to focus on the following:

k) Trends and Themes

l) What are competitors doing to be as successful as they are?

m) What could you do to make your business better?

E. **Organization and Management-**

n) Shares information on how your company will be structured and who will run it.

o) Describes the legal structure. Will your business be operated as a C or an S corporation?

p) Will your business be a sole proprietor or limited liability company (LLC)

F. **Service or product line**

q) What product will your company be selling, and what services you will offer?

r) What benefits will consumers get from your product?

s) Share your plans concerning; Intellectual property, and copyright or patented filings.

G. **Marketing and Sales**

t) What strategies and methods will you use to attract your consumers?

u) Describe ways your business will make sales.

v) What forms of advertisement will your company use?

H. **Financial projections-** When a business needs to prove to its audience its financial stability and success. In doing so it may include the following:

w) Include statements

x) Balance sheets

y) Cash flow statements for the last 3 to 5 years

z) List any collateral you could put against a loan

Explain your projections and make sure to line them up with your request for funding

Include any graphs or charts you may have that will visually explain the financial history of your business.

I. **Appendix-** A tool to use when supplying documents or other materials that may be requested. Items that you will want to include are the following:

1) Credit History

2) Resumes

3) Product Pictures

4) Letters of reference

5) License

6) Permits

7) Patents

8) Legal Documents

9) Other Documents

J. **<u>Customer relationships</u>**- The ways your customers interact with your business.

Automated or Personal
In-person or online

K. **<u>Revenue streams</u>**- In this section you'll want to thoroughly explain ways your business will generate money. Such as:

1) Direct Sales
2) Membership Fees
3) Selling Advertising Space
4) Social Media Streaming Services

Ways to Destroy Your Business Plan

When creating your business plan, you want to make sure you dot your "I's and cross all your "t's". This is important because any mistakes in your business plan that go unnoticed in your business plan preparation and presentation will undermine the credibility of the plan and hurt your chances to receive funding:

- Submitting a "rough copy," that is sloppy and filled with stains.
- Possessing outdated financial information or unrealistic industry comparisons.
- Failure to realize prospective pitfalls.
- Unknowledgeable about financial information.
- A plan that includes vague statements of strategy or does not provide important details.
- Not having some equity capital invested in the business.
- Starting the plan with unrealistic loan amounts or terms. Do your homework and propose a realistic structure.
- Too much focus on collateral.

Words of Encouragement for Stepping Into Your Millions!

Believe that all things are possible and that you will be that successful business owner living the life of your dreams. It will and can happen for you. You just have to be determined that nothing and no one will get in the way of what you are trying to achieve. It takes courage to step out in faith and go for it no matter what the nay-sayers think! When you hear negative comments regarding your dreams, ignore them, keep your head up, and keep stepping!

Remember you are on a mission and there is a greater reward waiting for you if you stick with it! You can have anything that you desire if you keep your faith and trust in God. After all, he is in control of your destiny. Every time a negative thought comes to your mind or any doubt shows up in your thoughts kick those thoughts out immediately! Tell yourself you can do this! You've got this! Don't let negative thoughts live in your min rent-free! NO NO NO!!

There is too much money to be made out here! Stop letting people make you feel like you are not enough. You're all that and then some! Remind yourself of that and keep stepping! So no more excuses no more hesitation, and no more procrastination! It's time to step into your future of Entrepreneurship. You know the saying…tomorrow is not promised to any of us. Now is the time to act!

Don't look to the right or the left. Keep stepping towards your millions!

The Significance of Meditation

Meditation can give you a sense of calm, peace, and balance that can lead to your emotional well-being and your overall health. Meditation can help carry you calmly through your day as well as help you manage certain medical conditions. Using mediation is helpful during stressful and overwhelming times.

Meditating keeps the mind clear and the thoughts positive. People who meditate can live happier lives than those who don't. Meditation is known to enhance the flow of constructive thoughts and positive emotions. Even a few minutes spent meditating regularly can make a big difference. Sometimes it's important to stop and breathe when you start to feel anxious or worked up. And trust me starting a new business can bring on lots of *anxiety, and stress*. ***But hopefully in a good way!***

Moreover, you don't have to adhere to religion to practice meditation. it's about developing calmness, practicing awareness, and decluttering the mind. Out with the negative thoughts and in with the positive ones. Additionally, meditation is very important and will open up doors in your life. Meditation is something God created. Read Joshua chapter 1 verse 8. Hence, meditation has been around for a long time. In the next section, I will share a meditation technique I learned that worked for me and hopefully will work for you!

Helpful Meditation Techniques To Use

When you get up in the morning before starting your day do the following:

1. Create a quiet place for your meditation.

2. Remove your shoes and sit down on either a chair or the floor to get comfortable. You may use some sort of yoga mat if you want. It is important to know that in preparing for your meditation make sure you choose a time where you will not be disturbed. This is what I like to call my time with God. Here I can release my troubles, situation problems, or issues I may be dealing with at the time. Or, I can use this time to quietly connect spiritually with my heavenly father.

3. Take a couple of minutes to do the breathing method of breathing in and out. I would do this until I felt at peace. It is always better to clear your mind when meditating. In doing so you can block out any distractions that may try to creep into your thoughts.

4. As you begin to meditate reflect on anything in your life you desire to get rid of. Then tell God all about it. Tell him your wants and desires. Whatever you believe, believe it will happen for you!

5. When talking to God in your meditation, you need to say these words, Father I am your child and I'm coming to you asking……and God will do just like that what you ask of him.

God tells us in his word to call those things were not as though they already were. In other words, you thank him in advance for answering your prayer. "Father I thank you for that new job!" The same thing goes for calling out a house, land, your Boaz, Finacial help, and whatever else your need or want from him.

If you have the faith and the courage to believe it, then expect to receive it upon asking! Do this daily for 30 days and nights and you will begin to see changes happening for you! And if you don't believe or trust this works, then I dare you to try God by his words. He will honor his words. All you have to do is let go and let God!

Remember this: meditation is time and space between you and God. It's a spiritual connection between you and him. And sometimes when we are stressed and going through hardships mentally, physically, or spiritually, meditation is the key. All you need to do is go into that secret place and tell God what it is you need for him to do for you. God will honor his word. In his word, he tells us to meditate day and night and we will have success.

Positive Scriptures Feeds the Mind and the Soul

There are many scriptures in the bible that speak on wealth and prosperity. In fact, throughout the entire Bible, we are taught principles, words to speak over our finances, and prayers to pray when we need a little bit of faith to get us through. Now you may be wondering how this applies to stepping into your destiny and following your dream of becoming a successful millionaire. Let me briefly explain. First off let me start by saying that I believe that by putting God at the forefront of all that we do, we can only succeed in doing it.

There is a particular scripture that lets us know that if we please the Lord and do what he asks, not only will he give us what we desire in our hearts, he said he would not withhold any good thing from us! **Psalm 37:4** Sometimes I read this scripture when I need to be reminded of what God promises when I do my part. There is nothing he wouldn't bless me to have or achieve.

Being an entrepreneur comes with its achievements and its setbacks. Having experienced this a time or two myself, the setbacks can be tough to bounce back from. However, when I need a reminder that no matter how bad things may look on the outside, there is a greater force at play working on my behalf. Therefore, I read **Romans 8:28** this scripture lets me know that ALL things are working together for my good. Hence, I don't need to worry.

Now another important scripture that has helped me in my entrepreneurship is **James 2:26** Having success with any business takes hard work, dedication, motivation, and faith! As of matter of fact, it is a total faith walk from the time you dared to dream of being an entrepreneur to the time you turned a dream into a reality. For faith to work, it requires taking action. You must first believe you can be an entrepreneur. Then, you do what it takes to become one! I strongly recommend applying scriptures daily to your personal life and your business. In doing so you feed your mind and your soul!

Final Thoughts.....................

Having prosperity means your needs are met. Whatever you want in your heart you have access to it. Therefore, not worrying about your needs causes you to live comfortably in your prosperity. You may have a lot of money but are you prosperous? Do you obtain riches outside of wealth? When you wear the suit of prosperity people want to be in your presence. Why? because they too desire prosperity in their own lives. Of course, wanting prosperity and gaining prosperity are two different things. You can want something from now until eternity. You must do what is necessary to achieve the very thing you want. In doing so remember these final thoughts.

Keep negative emotions under control. Negative energy brings negative outcomes. Surround yourself with positive people who bring positive energy. Get rid of delinquent people. Prosperous people do not engage with delinquent people.

Fear can be the greatest hindering block when it comes to reaching your full potential in gaining wealth and prosperity. Know who you are. If you know who you are you won't be a stumbling block to yourself or others.

Charity begins at home. Prosperity comes when you are a giver. Give in love and serve with a happy heart. Love yourself. In loving yourself take care of your well-being. Do things in moderation. Stay away from harmful substances such as drugs, and alcohol. These things can destroy your body.

Prosperity is important for generational family wealth and legacy. Therefore, you must protect your children and be mindful of the company they keep. Sometimes the so-called friends of your children can dilute your prosperity which can be a problem for you and your family's wealth in the future. Prosperity and wealth can be yours if reach out and grab hold of it!!